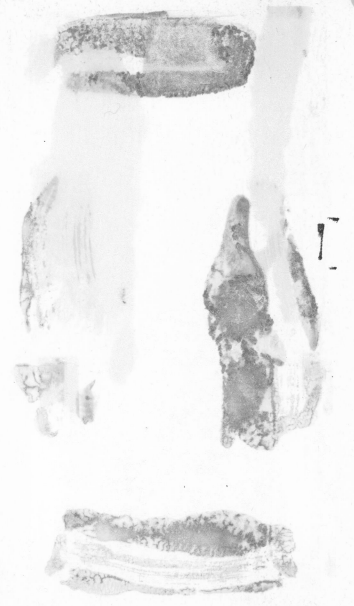

Modern Artists

Max Ernst

Harry N. Abrams, Inc., Publishers, New York

Werner Spies

Max Ernst

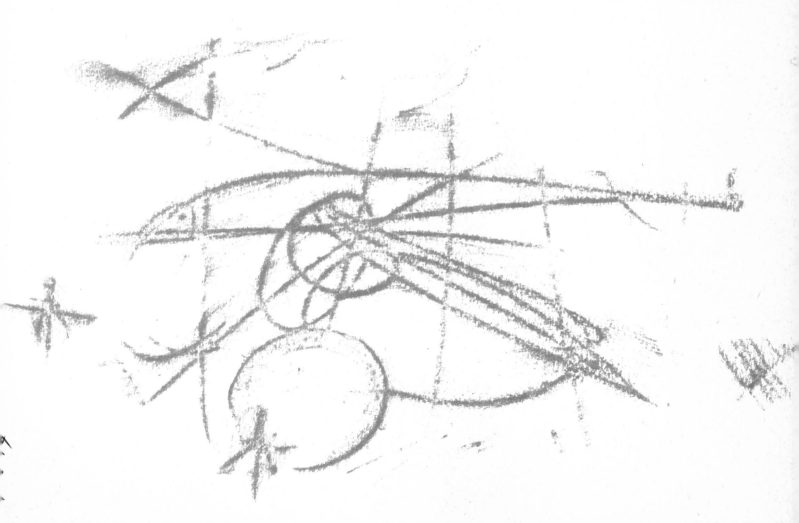

Translated from the German by Joseph M. Bernstein

Library of Congress Catalog Card Number: 69-12795

We know the exact day it happened. On August 10, 1925, in a hotel room in Pornic on France's Atlantic coast, Max Ernst discovered the technique of frottage.[1] Ernst's account of this event[2] sounds so convincing that we forget only too easily that such exactitude is usually a cover for skillful mystification. Indeed, everyone who has hitherto written about Ernst has accepted his story of the discovery of the frottage technique as gospel truth. That is, they have failed to distinguish between his sudden interest in the possibilities of frottage and the formal—even to some extent antipictorial—postulates of that technique. For we must not assume from Ernst's version that the frottage technique, so much a part of him, was merely a lucky accident. A look at his oeuvre produced before that August day in 1925 indicates we must delve more deeply into that chronicle of an act of creation. The prehistory of frottage lies buried beneath the countless details from which we can learn something about Ernst's approach to materials and media.

Ernst's story makes the technical side sound mysterious. He omits the subtle technical aspects of frottage—undoubtedly for philosophical and aesthetic reasons—and stresses its automatism. Moreover, as early as 1919 Ernst had prepared a number of sheets which—if we insist on the 1925 date—we may call frottages *avant la lettre*. He created these works, of which only scattered examples are extant,[3] in the Cologne printing house where, in 1919, he did the eight lithographs for *Fiat Modes*.[4] The circumstances under which these works appeared are interesting. They reveal parallels to the actual "discovery" of frottage Ernst launched six years later. We shall return to these works,[5] to which the frottage technique owes its initial impulse. Actually, however, they stand in contrast to Ernst's "classical" frottage.

In his "Au-delà de la peinture" Ernst has noted how he came to this rubbing technique—as a result of his fascination with the grain of a wood floor. Preceding his description is a commentary on a passage in Leonardo da Vinci's *Treatise on Painting*. Leonardo, so Vasari tells us, had an argument with Botticelli. Botticelli, who held landscape study in low esteem, asserted that to achieve the loveliest landscape all one had to do was to toss a color-soaked sponge against a wall. That recipe may be all right for a landscape subordinate to the theme of the painting—a kind of loosely defined, formless structure. But it is far from adequate if the meaning of a landscape has to be captured in detail. Hence, in his dispute with Botticelli Leonardo introduces the concept of composition. He was concerned with more closely defining the formless structure of the spot of color and retouching it so intensively that it would awaken predetermined associations in the eyes of the beholder. Here we have two things at opposite poles: the painter's freedom, open to the inspiration of a formless, open structure, and the viewer's predetermined vision, forced by the painter to recognize a well-defined structure. This contrast between utmost freedom in the act of creativity and utmost determinateness in the completed work plays a large part in Ernst's art. (For that reason it is exciting to trace the boundary between automatism and determinateness in his work.) Leonardo was not content with merely bringing decorative ornaments to a painting; he sought to create a psychological response that, to quote André Chastel—the first to point out this parallel between Leonardo and Max Ernst—answers "the inner pulsation of the soul and the inexhaustible vitality of nature."[6]

Here let me quote from Ernst's own account: "On August 10, 1925, I was seized with an unbearable visual need to discover the technical means whereby this theory of Leonardo's is clearly worked out in practice. It began with a . . . childhood memory, in the course of which an imitation mahogany board in my bed played the part of the optical provocateur in a daydream. On a rainy evening I found myself in a hotel on the French coast when I was gripped by an obsession that made me stare excitedly at the deeply grooved cracks in the floorboards. I decided to yield to the symbolism of this obsession. To sustain my potential for meditation and hallucination, I made a series of sketches on the floorboards by arbitrarily placing a few sheets of paper on them and then began to rub on them with a black pencil. When I closely scrutinized the sketches thus made—'the dark areas and other, delicately lit half-dark areas'—I was amazed at the sudden intensification of my visionary capabilities and the hallucinatory result of the contrasting pictures."

This passage is written in a way that reminds one strongly of Ernst's description of his discovery of collage. The latter text begins: "On a rainy day in 1919, when I found myself in a village on the Rhine. . . ."[7] In both cases the conscious use of a new technique is presented as a discovery. Not until we study the text more closely do we realize that this discovery was not without prior assumptions. It is fused with sudden memories that had been overlaid with other impressions. So the "discovery" really boils down to this: the artist clearly *sees* an essential feature of his consciousness. Collage or frottage are "discoveries" that immediately profit by a predisposition on the part of the person who puts them to work.

Frottage may be considered a completely autonomous technique of Ernst's. It seems to have been strictly limited to him, for the influences it has exerted are slight and almost solely of a technical nature.[8] But collage, as Ernst practiced it, must be sharply differentiated from the collage of the Cubists. The difference can be reduced to a very simple formula, which also points to the problem that arises here: to the Cubists collage is a technique, a formal method; it belongs to the painter's palette. To Max Ernst it is an iconographic element. The latter statement is true of frottage as well. From the very outset frottage was more than a technique, as the almost mystical tone in Ernst's account of it emphasizes; it was something different from the invention of the lithograph or the watercolor. Frottage is bound up with a new objectivity. It creates this objectivity in that the structure Ernst rubs through is subordinate to a pictorial object that has nothing to do with that structure. Two planes of reality coincide. A structure that refers a priori to something unrelated to the pictorial object, that at first glance does not seem adequate, encounters the pictorial object

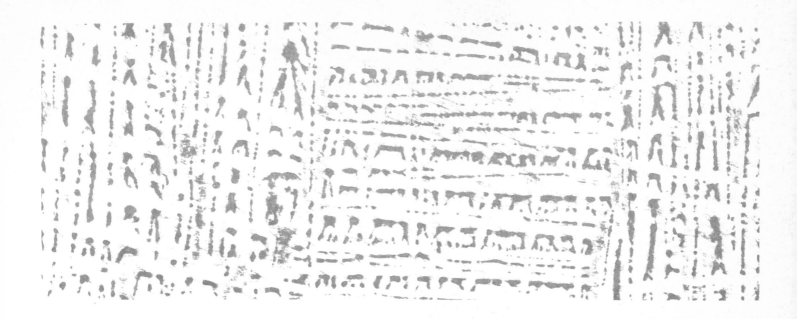

that has hitherto never been expressed in extrapictorial structural elements. Now the grained texture of a floor, for example, replaces the stroke of a brush or pen. This apparent illogic creates the curious state of suspension in which Ernst's figures live. Even where we do not clearly understand the structure, it is not fully integrated with the object.

The contradiction between realistic or Surrealistic theme and the new treatment remains. It exists against the background of our historical knowledge of painting and drawing. If we seek to relate the discovery of frottage technique to the general artistic movement and the premise from which it proceeded, we find that the confrontation of two planes of reality leads us right to the definition of Surrealism. Here there is not a single stroke that at the same time does not point to the iconographic concept fusing theme and execution in such a way that the ambiguity becomes more powerfully deliberate. As a result, in Ernst's *Histoire Naturelle* (1925)—the first and most comprehensive cycle of his frottages—he calls into question the rational and the explicable, which is the aim of a natural history; through a slight stroke of the hand he again renders inexplicable and indescribable the world as explained and described. Here, too, we must again refer to Leonardo, whose discovery of *sfumato* was more than an achievement of technique. It created a very specific, conceptual kind of painting, possible only in a specific iconographic framework.

To the artist frottage is not only a technique in which two object-planes overlap and penetrate each other; it is also a means by which he frees himself from his inhibitions. Indeed, we know of virtually no other artist's life in which everything, from childhood on, has been so resolutely set up as a defense against the artistic and the pictorial. Ernst's "calling" as an artist is the story of a complicated and sophisticated detour. This path led past the destruction of the artistic in the traditional sense. Ernst's encounter with Dada and the sharp reaction of the people of Cologne to his iconoclastic forays attest to this. The discovery of frottage might be labeled an attempt to get back to painting by the back door, so to speak. Ernst needed a medium that would rid him of timidity in the face of what he considers the supreme arrogance: the confrontation of artist and empty canvas. Even in frottage the impulse of the Dadaist is still discernible. He proceeds from a nonartistic reality. He converts Duchamp's Ready-Made into graphic terms. But he does not stop there. The reality he rubbed onto his sheet becomes a way of stimulating inspiration. Horror of the void plays its part in this. In Ernst's own words, when he faces the white sheet of paper he is seized with a virginity complex. Ernst cannot begin with brush strokes. To overcome his shyness he has to resort to little devices. Throughout his oeuvre we come upon problems he set for himself—in almost every work one detects a tiny trace of frottage or collage. At present Ernst feels that, from the psychological viewpoint, this fear of the void was one of the reasons why he made "at least something out of it."

From his comments on theory we learn that what concerns Ernst most is bringing controlled and uncontrolled activity into balance. The fantasy in the sheets of *Histoire Naturelle* may be overwhelming, but Ernst has done his utmost to make the end product equivocal; the automatism that brings about this cosmogony is kept under control. Ernst has provided his sheets with a guarantee that ensures clarity and immediacy.

These works were created at a time when the Surrealists, using various media and automatic writing, tried repeatedly to set everything in motion in order to "make their souls monstrous" (Rimbaud). Frottage is Ernst's contribution to automatism. He himself believes that frottage is the equivalent of literary automatism. As the creator devotes himself to this activity (or passivity), as he limits his own co-operation with increasing rigorousness, he himself finally becomes the onlooker. This comment was made at a time when automatism was considered the *ne plus ultra* of authentic expression. When one gauges the results Ernst attained with the help of frottage and especially with the technique of grattage as transferred to the canvas, one is bound to conclude that the automatic nature of these works was overrated in the theoretical writings of the period. Even in the theory of Surrealism one notes a gradual modification of the doctrine of "automatic writing." André Breton, who, with Philippe Soupault, seized upon automatic writing, owes much less to that method than has hitherto been supposed. Like other Surrealists, he was so fascinated by the results of Robert Desnos' texts as spoken in a sleeping state, that he wanted to verify psychic automatism in himself. The First Surrealist Manifesto (1924) tells of these efforts, but they were exaggerated in order to illustrate the definition of Surrealism

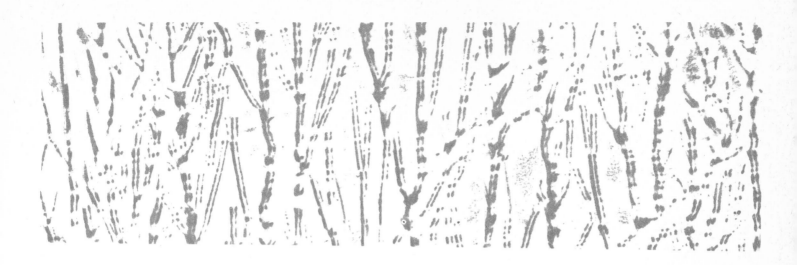

toward which Breton was heading. Nevertheless the chief works—the First Manifesto, the writings about painting, and Breton's *Nadja*—are the result of thoughtful formulation. Indeed, *Nadja* is a superb example of how to simulate a Surrealist effect that lies altogether outside the realm of language. *Nadja* is a report, a Veristic record. Its unique effect springs from the fact that there is a vast discrepancy between the depicter and what he depicts. In his essay *Le Message automatique* (1933)[9] Breton basically admits that the naïve type of automatism failed to yield important results: "I am not afraid to say that the story of *écriture automatique* in Surrealism has been one of constant misfortune."

Ernst's *Histoire Naturelle* appeared a year after the publication of the First Surrealist Manifesto, which included virtually no mention of painting. Hence his account of the origins of frottage bears a slightly polemical character. Ernst thus seeks to correct the omission from Breton's manifesto—at the same time making use of the latter's vocabulary. Actually, until the appearance of the frottages in *Histoire Naturelle*, Breton could only speak qualifiedly of Surrealist painting. He set only one requirement for the graphic transcription of the hallucinatory picture: "It is not a question of drawing; one must simply break off." In his *Histoire Naturelle* Ernst fulfills this requirement. Of course, with him "breaking off" is not merely an automatic way of bringing about a completely uncontrollable and unstructured mood. With Ernst, the reflex that occurs sorts the automatically won material and structures it into semantic units. Repetition, variation, exchange of systems of relationships within the sheets, one form referring to another—all this illustrates how *Histoire Naturelle* transforms the automatically won material into a language. This language, as we have said, doubles the language of things. Hence the titles Ernst gives his works.[10] Often they are ironic and function as a control. This style and concept of a work of art parallels what Maurice Blanchot has said about the poet Lautréamont. Blanchot stresses that Lautréamont's constant mockery, by which he called into question the sentence he had just written and, so to speak, crossed it out, became by this act of denial his critical consciousness.[11] By the same token it limited the automatic nature of Lautréamont's writing.

Surrealist painting strove increasingly to acquire an iconography. This was true above all in the case of Salvador Dali, who, like the Breton of *Nadja,* used a conventional, Veristic technique on unusual themes. In Dali this quickly led to formalism. His "paranoid-critical activity"[12] sought to connect Ernst's precisely delineated frottages and grattages with Leonardo's discussion about the interpretation of spots of color or crumbling walls. But Dali banned all freedom from his photographically exact pictures, thus anticipating the result of the interpretation and prescribing the paranoid states in minute detail.

The first frottages mentioned above—"premature" frottages, as it were—are dated 1919, the year in which Ernst was fascinated by the pictures in an illustrated catalogue of objects "intended for anthropological, microscopic, psychological, mineralogical, and paleontological experiments." The mysterious ubiquitousness of such diverse forms, incomprehensible in logical terms, produced in Ernst, in his own words,[13] a sudden intensification of his visionary faculties. The external world becomes overwhelming, the catalogue a résumé of the world at hand. All during the nineteenth century, of course, lists had been drawn up—but the factual flood streaming from the catalogue that had fallen into Ernst's hands no longer had anything to do with that kind of cataloguing. In Balzac such enumerations helped characterize people; they illuminated persons in their relation to things. This was not so with the lists Ernst chanced upon—lists no longer corresponding to any sociologically definable reality. They no longer characterize an individual—any more than do the series of pages in Joyce's *Ulysses* constituting the catalogue of a mail-order furniture company. They put an end to concentration on a specific interior, yet they afford one the possibility at any moment of seeking a new solution, by virtue of this very availability. In Joyce the interior becomes an unstable thing; in Ernst the juxtaposition of disparate objects quickens the loss of faith in the unequivocal evidence of objects. (In "Au-delà de la peinture" Ernst tells of earlier experiences as a child, which demonstrated to him that reality is merely a visual deception of familiar things by which we safeguard ourselves against the unknown.) Ernst's interest in natural history—another version of the mail-order catalogue—leads him to the theme of the frottages in his *Histoire Naturelle.* The point of departure for collages and frottages is the same.[14] In the print shop where in 1919 Ernst makes the lithographs for *Fiat Modes,* he is fascinated by wooden letters in type. He rubs the characters on paper. By superimposing, juxtaposing, and combining big and small letters he composes figures that conform to remotely anthropomorphic structures (page 2). The skeleton made of letters is not legible. It is not a construction, like a *"poème-objet,"*[15] that may have a XII

semantic meaning. On the contrary, by putting letters upside down or at a 90-degree angle, Ernst is trying to wrench them out of their prevailing context. The result, a forerunner of the frottage technique, is the expression of an unbiased encounter with type characters. These characters are designed for printing; but instead of bringing out their expressiveness by means of printer's ink, Ernst rubs in their forms with graphite on a sheet of paper. Thus their usual appearance is distorted: for instance, the asymmetrical *A* appears in reverse, as in a mirror image. Ernst works only with the forms; he makes compositions out of them but does not interpret them.[16] Therein lies the crucial difference between these compositions and the later frottages of *Histoire Naturelle*. He is still concentrating merely on objects he has recognized. The result is unequivocal, since the type blocks preserve their unity. At some points the composition of rubbed letters is enlarged with a pencil: joints are added, shadows indicated, the letters are modeled with subtle hatchings. In this way Ernst seeks to give the composition a kind of relief. Hence the results, though achieved by a technique reminiscent of printing, stem much less from printing than from the wood blocks themselves. Since in this composition the reality of the wood blocks is barely infringed upon, but rather is transferred to the sheet of paper by a *trompe-l'oeil* effect, we feel that it would be more correct to consider this work in connection with the collages. Ernst tells us he made approximately fifty such sheets, some of them colored. He sent them to a Dada exhibition in Berlin and never got them back.

There are numerous compositions from this period in which Ernst was prompted—as in the case of the sheet with the wood blocks—by on eor by several motives. The famous *The Hat Makes the Man* (page 34, b) was based on the juxtaposition of various hats cut out of a catalogue. Ernst completed the collage with pencil, ink, and watercolor. In this instance, too, the various techniques are kept apart: Just as the frottage parts of the wood-block compositions were differentiated from the sketched parts, so here collage, pencil, and watercolor are distinct. On this clear composition objects and connecting lines are differentiated with extreme accuracy. (We are reminded of what Marcel Duchamp achieved several years later in his *Large Glass*.) Because of this sharp differentiation, the viewer gets the illusion of a logical mechanism: the pseudo-machines and pseudo-functions, made up of strictly stereometric and clearly drawn forms, thus lend a kind of credibility to the over-all effect. In fact, they play on the mechanistic idea in such a way that the beholder unquestioningly accepts these objects as equipped with every guarantee of reliability.[17] We react similarly to the creatures and forms in *Histoire Naturelle*. As Veristic, logical details blend with the newly created and the unseen, pictures come to life that cause us to rub our eyes in amazement as we gaze at them. Yet we can hardly question the existence of these things in view of the true details in them. Ernst's experience with wood blocks in the print shop is but one aspect of his maturing creative activity. The many other works he created during this period go back ultimately to one of his favorite childhood books—*The Book of Inventions*.

Again we find mechanical elements everywhere: in his sketches, his collages, and in the first two sculptures—two reliefs—Ernst made out of various materials. Points of contact with Kurt Schwitters are obvious—but Ernst's works differ even externally from Schwitters' in their accuracy of execution. Ernst continued to experiment with the most widely diversified forms and materials. One of his most significant works, *Dadaville* (page 35, c), a relief in cork and plaster of Paris done in 1923–24, shows him moving toward a new surface structure. At first the effect he was later to achieve in his frottages seemed possible only in the field of sculpture; the roughened surface and disintegrating, irregular outer skin of the cork brought a new element to the sculpture of the period. But this work is not significant solely because for the first time it attempts to coarsen the entire surface (an effect Ernst later attained in painting as well, by using the technique of grattage, which is the frottage technique applied to oil painting). It is a key work, yet at the same time it produces one of the main motifs in Ernst's iconography: the verticals that form the petrified city or ridged forest. This is an archetypal form for him, the origin and meaning of which remain obscure. It reminds one of the Dicq, the breakwater on the island of Jersey, in front of which Victor Hugo had himself photographed and whose fissured form he reproduced in sketches. Here too we find a positive portion in the foreground alternating with a darker part lying in shadow. An apparently abstract figure, it drove Hugo to imagine figures in a thousand shapes and forms that are part of the web of life.

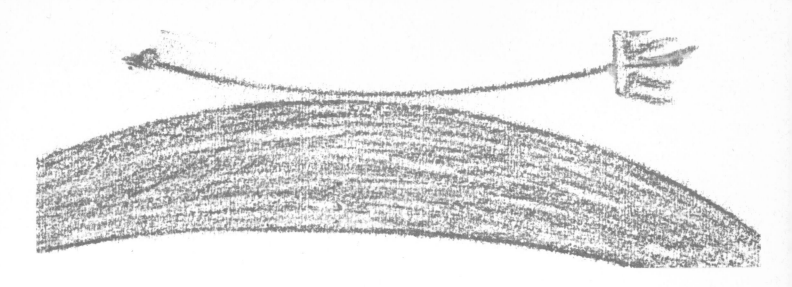

Dadaville, leading into the frottages of *Histoire Naturelle*, is a work the artist "interpreted": A structure was evolved—for the first time, in fact, a plastically comprehensible structure. Whereas *Fiat Modes*, with its abrupt perspectives *("troubles de perspectives")* and lines of flight rushing in various directions, is still reminiscent of Giorgio de Chirico's compositions,[18] in *Dadaville* Ernst creates a basic form from which he subsequently composes his own vision of the city. In *Dadaville* we have the first foundation-walls of the later *The Entire City*: it is the total city, in which even the smallest spot is disposed of. The horror of the void has gripped the city. Here are no vast empty squares as in De Chirico, no arcades surmounted by a clock that shows the self-same early afternoon hour. Ernst's metropolis is full and saturated—like a crystal.

Dadaville is but one example of a series of works Ernst did in the early 1920s, in all of which he sought to blast the material homogeneity of painting. In this respect the works in which the collage portions are subordinate to the drawing are particularly revealing. In *Perturbation, My Sister* (1921; page 35, a), for instance, the image of an automobile tire and the small chains that form a thick veil are not put into the painting as formal components; they are there to evoke matter rather than form in the spectator—and that was what led Ernst to frottage. The same is true of *Landscape to My Taste* (page 34, c). Here, according to his own testimony, Ernst reworked a photograph he took in the Eifel region of Germany, south of Düren, where he was mountain-climbing with Baargeld.[19]

His experience with structures derived from such variegated objects guided Ernst's creativity in a new direction. His rich fantasy, exploiting the unlikeliest objects, stimulated him to produce new pictures. His mind concentrated on what at first glance looked

like formless objects. Childhood memories—the imitation mahogany bedboard and the innumerable games and figures floating in the inexhaustible realm of a child's imagination—forced themselves time and again into his consciousness. Here we encounter a striking parallel to the creative process in Marcel Proust. He too was impelled to creative work after undergoing a specific sensory experience: the taste of a madeleine dipped in tea, for example. The involuntary memory catches hold of psychophysical details and brings back lost time. A reading of Waldberg's biography of Ernst[20] confirms that a great many themes appearing in Ernst's work in the 1920s were preshaped by childhood experiences. That is why a comparison with Proust's *Remembrance of Things Past* does not seem amiss, even though Proust's results differ from Ernst's in their rationalism. In the very first pages of *Swann's Way* we come upon Proust's method, similar in detail to Ernst's: Proust lies in his cork-lined room, insulated against the outside world. Ernst had retired to a hotel room on the French Atlantic coast. Proust awakens in the night, no longer knowing where he is. As he tries to get his bearings, the darkness fills him with memories. He finds his way back to specific reminiscences. Ernst's technique, like Proust's, proceeds from initial stimulation: his involuntary memory seizes upon the grainings in the washed floor boards and leads back to things and events that had previously been in his fantasy as a child.

Dadaville, a mixture of natural phenomenon and interpreted immaterial form, belongs thematically to the subsequent frottage cycle of *Histoire Naturelle*. How exciting it is to leaf quickly through the illustrations of these works and see the well-known mingle with the exotic, the obvious with the unbelievable. Somehow this cycle of illustrations leads one into the unusual and the Surreal. XVIII

The illustrations for the *Encyclopédie* of Diderot and d'Alembert include drawings under the heading of "Natural History" that seek to broaden the concept of nature in the *Encyclopédie* with the help of natural phenomena—that concept having been unduly restricted to the cosmological and theological level. This accounts for Ernst's attempt to draw as many phenomena as possible that approach the visual. The double-page engraving, *The Giant's Causeway in Antrim County, Ireland,* is one of the most striking examples of this. Another "natural" example would be the symmetrical stone cylinders of volcanic origin vertically arranged in the structure of *Dadaville*. These are also related to the exceptional situations Ernst presented in his *Histoire Naturelle*.[21]

The series of thirty-four frottages published by Jeanne Bucher in Paris in 1926, a year after they were finished, in collotype and in an edition of three hundred copies, is thus entitled *Histoire Naturelle* (pages 4–28). With Paul Eluard, Ernst had selected the frottages that basically constituted this edition. For financial reasons no more sheets could be included. Then, from the remaining works, Eluard put together a private *Histoire Naturelle*.[22] Individual sheets, dealing with the same general themes, fell into various hands.

If we limit ourselves to the collection of thirty-four sheets, we are immediately struck by the systematic division of the series. The sheets are divided into groups. These may be described as follows:

1. Cosmogonic-cosmic sheets (pages 4–7)

2. Plantlike sheets (pages 10, 11, 14–16)

3. Animal sheets (pages 21, 23–25)

4. Anthropomorphic sheets (pages 26, 27)

5. Human, mystical sheet (*Eve;* page 28)

Does this breakdown include all the frottages in the cycle? Among the sheets not included in the edition of *Histoire Naturelle* are mainly variants of the five themes listed above. However, there are also important sheets for which there are no equivalents in *Histoire Naturelle*. Among these is—we are quoting from the most complete edition extant of the frottages in *Histoire Naturelle*[23] —*The Earth Is a Distant Woman* (page 35, b), the simplest structure within this cycle. Two horizontal surfaces arranged in parallel fashion are overlaid by a narrow vertical form containing three holes. Here the basic plan is somewhat different from the one we recognize in the collage *The Little Tear Gland That Says Tic Tac* (1920; page 34, d). The theme of repetition of an infrastructure in the frottage is doubled in the collage by repeating a comprehensible structure. Missing, furthermore, from *Histoire Naturelle* is the characteristic sheet *Easy*, which depicts a bird's head twice—once in a naturalistic vein and a second time in a more abstract-geometric drawing. This dualism of naturalistic and geometric form also characterizes the sheet *The Origin of the Clock* (page 29), only the more naturalistic form (page 23) of which was included in the printed edition. *The Calendar of Performances* (page 31) was also omitted. One of the most significant syntheses Ernst undertook in his *Histoire Naturelle* was to link the archetype of *The Entire City*, an Acropolis type of city, with a cosmic representation of the heavens. Also among the sheets left out are *Tropical Trophies* and *The Apple of Concord* (page 32). They imitate works done the previous year, in which Ernst was already using the frottage technique, albeit as a means of contrast. In one of these earlier works, *Two Grapes* (page 36a), he contrasts the positive, watercolor form with the negative, rubbed form—grapes as *trompe-l'oeil* and grapes as monochrome shadows in frottage. In the other, *Visible Apple* (page 36, b), the contrast is even more marked. Here the pear-shaped flat shadow extending behind the apple matches the apple's positive and actual form. In this case too, frottage is used purely as a means of contrast. In these early works, therefore, Ernst resolved the dialectical antithesis of presence-absence by contrasting two different technical methods. Thus, in *The Beautiful Gardener* (1923/24; page 36, c), a plastically portrayed figure is set off against a drawn one. In *Black Pigeon and Pale Pigeon* (1925), the contrast between the two planes of reality is noticeable even in the title. In *Visible Apple*, on the other hand, the structure of the frottage elements has only a general meaning; it indicates a negative presence in the picture as a whole. The over-all form acts as foil. The two examples cited from *Histoire Naturelle* repeat the experiment Ernst made in *Two Grapes* and *Visible Apple*, in a fully developed technical medium—frottage; yet they remain the only ones in which Ernst himself distinguishes between positive and negative form by using frottage. The really negative form for frottage is white space. *Caesar's Palette* (page 19) is an example of how the theme of presence and absence is solved with the help of the dialectics of frottage and the white space on the sheet.

The plane of illusion in *Histoire Naturelle* has not been breached. This thoroughly monistic formulation derives from the fact that

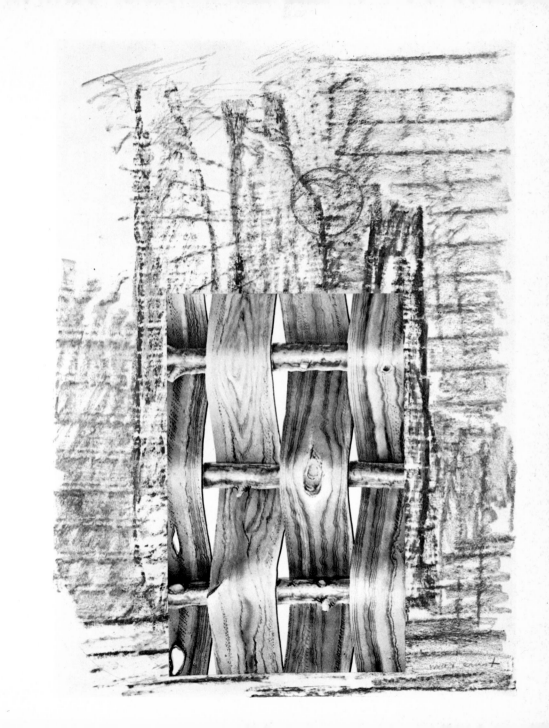

the various structures Ernst rubbed were treated as equal in rank. The materials in question lose their independent character. Wood, string, leather, crumpled paper, stale bread, thread—and whatever else is placed beneath the sheet—undergo a transformation. Ernst equalizes the individual materials. Where this is not possible he makes them look peculiar by arranging them in a way that reveals nothing of their real structural basis. In the course of these works the rubbed material is used with increasing freedom. Of course, at first the natural structure remains in the foreground. In *Shaving the Walls* (page 17), the first sheet Ernst executed, the floor structure is actually palpable. (In the *Histoire Naturelle* series this sheet appears as plate 21.) Here wood becomes the wooden partition: the changeover is by no means metaphorical. We remain strictly within the same material domain. Behind the wooden boards a small twig appears; the arrangement we saw in *Visible Apple* is here switched. The positive, almost realistically drawn form of the sheets lies spatially behind the vague structure of the wood.

Leonardo's wall, against which Botticelli tossed a color-soaked sponge, stands—as a wooden partition—at the outset of Ernst's work on *Histoire Naturelle*. The title of the sheet, *Shaving the Walls*, describes the technical process of frottage: the artist's crayon "shaves the walls" as it passes across the wood. Ernst seizes upon the theme: the material in question appears on the sheet. It has not yet been transposed; it is still—like Botticelli's spot of color—open to diverse interpretations.[24] Still, Ernst was not content with rubbing the wood graining and interpreting its initially amorphous structure graphically. In the course of his work on *Histoire Naturelle* he created a whole list of objects he placed under the paper.[25] Here we note two different sources of inspiration, one of them more structural in character. As in the case of the floor boards in the hotel room, Ernst is fascinated by the open, ambiguous structure of an object which, as he works over it, he transforms into a graphically fixed form. In these instances he uses the wood graining, the hard crust of bread, the granulation of leather, or the plaiting of a straw hat as abstract material subject to specific form. His task is to synchronize the material at hand with a form. A wooden floor turns into a turbulent ocean surface (page 5); a thick layer of oil paint (page 7) to which Ernst has given a wavelike motion by means of a comb becomes the Gulf Stream; the scaly structure of a straw hat changes into a cypress tree (page 10); rubbed threads become scars or horses (page 25). The other source of inspiration involves the form of the rubbed object: this method leaves the object intact and, as in a collage, includes it unchanged in the work. This occurs, for example, where he simply rubs a tiny shell (page 11) or the leaves of a chestnut tree (page 21), or where a small piece of bread becomes half a loaf (page 22).

As we have seen, the rubbed structures undergo various transformations in the course of the work. The structure is not graphically set until the work acquires specific pictorial coherence. This holds good for both kinds of frottage technique: the first type, which simply derives from structures; and the second type, which brings structure and form to the sheet in one stroke. Thus the same structure that springs from the graining in a piece of wood can at one time signify the ocean (page 5) and at another time the earth (page 8). In this way Ernst prevents the viewer from arriving at overhasty visual conclusions. The graphic language remains ambiguous and flexible, thus avoiding the danger of pictorial nominalism, in which every structure might stick to the object like a label.

If one looks at these sheets, one is struck by their formal unity. One feels that Ernst has stressed identity of form and structure at the expense of the distinctive value of the structures themselves. A comparison of *Histoire Naturelle* with his previous work confirms this. We encounter a good many themes prefigured in earlier works. It is instructive to note that in his *Histoire Naturelle* Ernst has made allowances for the new technical medium by a calculated choice of his stock of forms. *The Fascinating Cypress* (page 10) offers an especially interesting example of just such a carry-over. This is the upside-down botanical version of the painting *Ubu Imperator,* adjusted to a system of relationships with strict perspective.

There are few overlappings in the sheets of *Histoire Naturelle.* The graphic, incisive character is sustained in virtually every sheet. Only in a few instances does the arrangement of structures and forms or the organization of space become complicated. The most complicated sheet remains *The Calendar of Performances* (page 31). Over-all, we note two different systems in the sheet distribution. One renounces central perspective, locating structures above one another—generally in a horizontal arrangement. This system is reserved above all for the cosmic and cosmological sheets (pages 4, 7). Because of the horizontal arrangement the space dimension remains boundless, thus serving as a symbol of infinity. The other system, which Ernst used as early as 1919 in his illustrations for *Fiat Modes,*[26] creates space by placing various fixed points one behind the other. De Chirico's careening perspectives, which fascinated Ernst, live on here in a simplified and systematized form. In *The Pampas* (page 8) the tree in the background is repeated twice, each time sharply reduced, so that these fixed points simulate an expanse of space. The same method—the first figure in the foreground of the drawing being repeated in the background in greatly reduced form—may be found in numerous other works (pages 9–11). In size, the ratio between the figure in the foreground and its reduction in the background is approximately 7 : 1. In this way the space is objectified; it seems measurable. One sheet, however, reveals a departure from this arrangement in perspective: In *Come into the Continents* (page 20), the figures have been drawn against a horizon that is totally blank. The scenery is so abstract that one can scarcely discern whether the sheet represents interior or exterior space. Three forms—glasslike structures—which from our experience with central perspective we would judge to be of equal size are arranged on a surface. The largest glass, which instinctively we relate to the foreground, is here in the mid-area. In the foreground and background are two other glasses reduced in perspective relative to the glass in the mid-area. Hence there is a double perspective in the picture. The

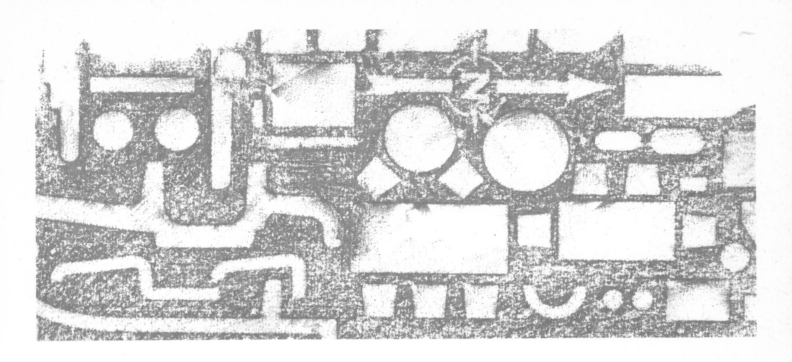

viewer concentrates on the mid-area and then looks fore and aft. The glass in the background casts a shadow against an imaginary wall. Suddenly the space becomes an interior: a solid framework seems to enclose the stage on which the three glasses stand.

The third space concept one identifies in these frottages is the stage. In the final analysis it is a variant of the space system of central perspective. In many sheets objects fill virtually the entire surface, space shrinking to a small area (pages 16, 18, 19). The dialectical counterpart to the broad, almost unlimited space perspective emerges. In *The Origin of the Clock* the theme of narrowness is expressed in a poetic image: a bird flutters, imprisoned between two walls. The concept of freedom, of boundlessness, collides with the amorphous, immovable prison of the walls. The endless arc that the bird describes while flying in the sky becomes here a fluttering to-and-fro movement. Eternity, thus imprisoned, becomes time; the fluttering to and fro articulates timelessness, turning into the swing of a pendulum.

The essence of *Histoire Naturelle* is revealed to us in the coupling of completely accessible meanings—usually the realistic portrayal of a being or "natural" phenomenon—with unknown meanings that can only be grasped poetically. Tiny changes make the known monstrous. The individualization of natural things transforms objective seeing into imaginative vision. In these sheets Ernst has

created numerous prototypes not only for his own work but also for our ability to give up syntheses and isolate facts. This ability to individualize, to enjoy a world of monstrosities, to fasten on a single eye, an imprisoned bird, two horses rubbing noses, or the seismographic chart of an earthquake, can lead us to the Surreal just as surely as can the exaggerated piling up of every detail imaginable. Here the Surrealism of isolation contrasts with the synthetic works of Surrealism that crowd hundreds of details into a single picture—the baroque Surrealism of psychological satiety (Dali). Although we are confronted with individual objects, we do not manage to solve the sense of hallucination in the individualized figures.

The theme Ernst developed in *Histoire Naturelle* may be found in many variations in his subsequent paintings. But the influence of *Histoire Naturelle* was not limited solely to Ernst's iconography. While he was working on *Histoire Naturelle,* frottage evolved into so sure and flexible a technique [27] that it was an altogether logical step to carry it over into oil painting. That is how grattage developed from frottage. As formerly in the case of the drawing paper, so now the canvas repeats structures over which it is stretched. But grattage owes its effect to more than just the rubbed structure; the trelliswork of the canvas itself has its say. Unlike the drawing paper, the canvas does not remain merely a medium. The specific nature of its material, blending with another structure, causes it to become a component part of the painting. Ernst's first frottage on canvas was done in 1925. *Airplane Trap* (1935; page 36, d) is one of the most revealing examples. In it Ernst has actually assembled an inventory of the structures he used in his frottages and grattages: a small block of wood, a pattern for printing fabrics, corrugated tin. Later Ernst again developed frottage for mixed techniques. There are sheets in which watercolor, drawing, collage, and frottage have been simultaneously used (pages XV, XXI). Frottage technique appears also in his graphic works. Treating lithographic transfer-paper with frottage technique (page IX), Ernst gave lithography a new range of expression.[28] In recent years Ernst has turned again and more intensively to pure frottage. He has introduced a few important innovations that go beyond the technique as we know it from the sheets in *Histoire Naturelle*. Tinted paper, the use of colored pencils, grease crayons, pastels, red pencils, and charcoal (page XXVII) afford frottage a breadth of variation he had stopped striving for in *Histoire Naturelle*. The effect of the new sheets is more painterly, the composition is on a larger scale (page 36, e), the rhythm of the strokes has become freer and more widely meshed, inasmuch as colored grease crayons leave a softer mark than graphite. The emptiness that in many sheets of *Histoire Naturelle* counterbalances the presence of an individual theme and holds the pictorial image in suspense has disappeared from these later sheets. The new sheets are fuller. Something of the dense, painterly atmosphere of the grattages of recent years has carried over into them.

DIE ALEXANDER - SCHLACHT. 66

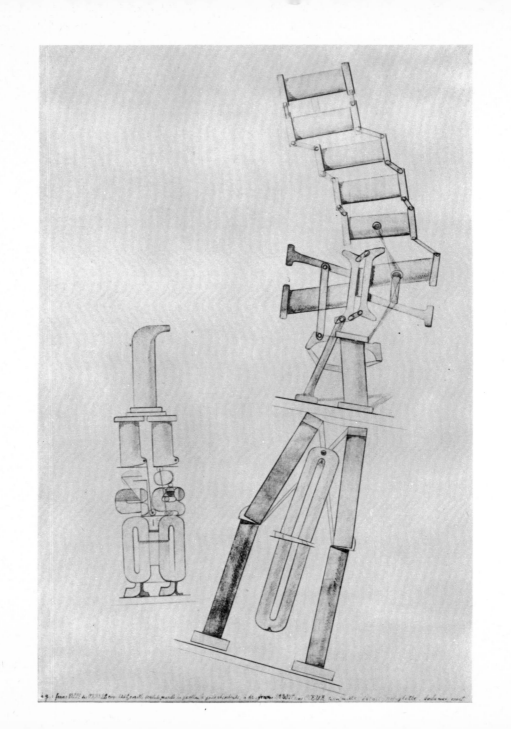

max ernst   erectio sine qua non

3

4

6

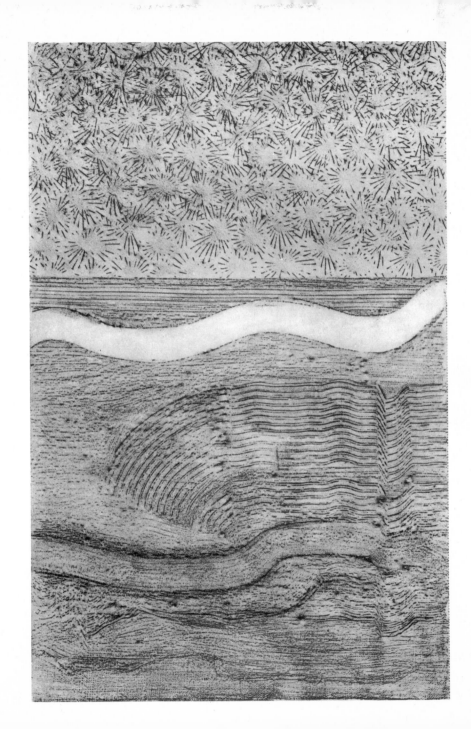

7

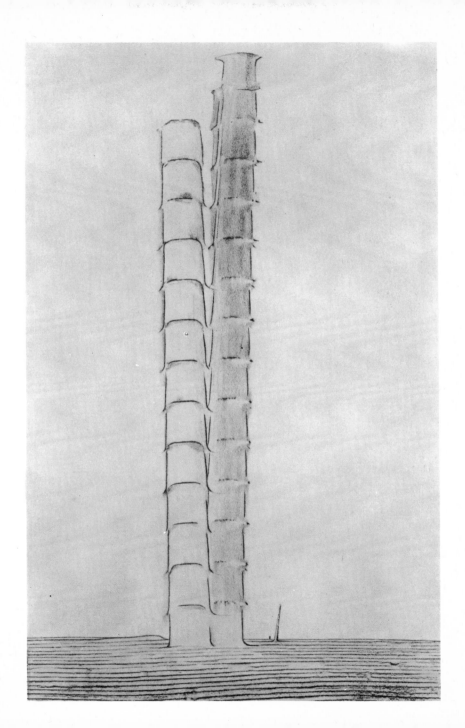

9

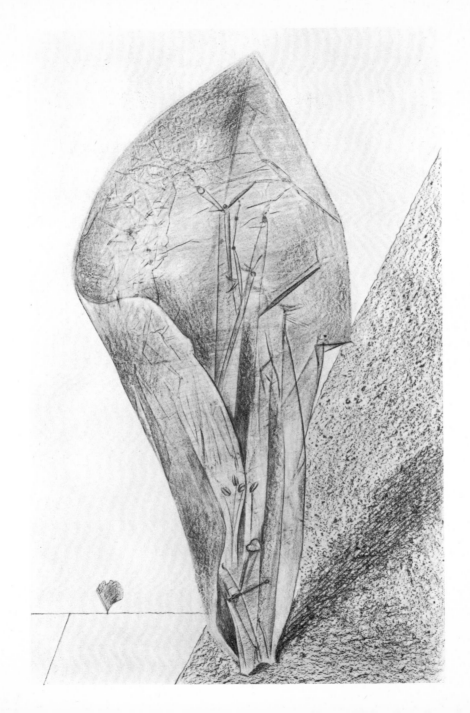

11

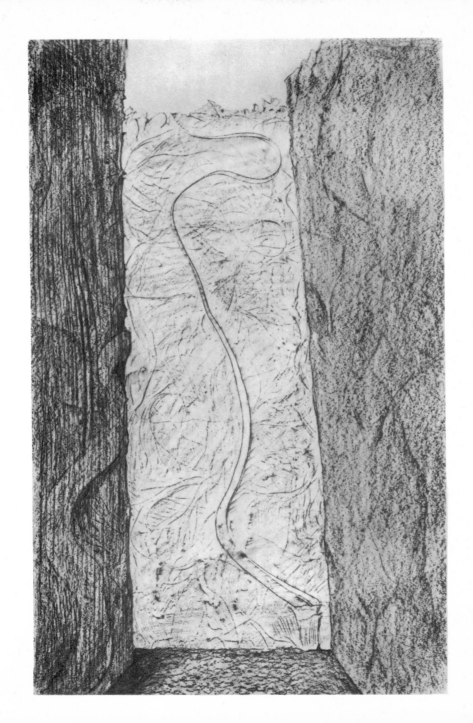

13

16

18

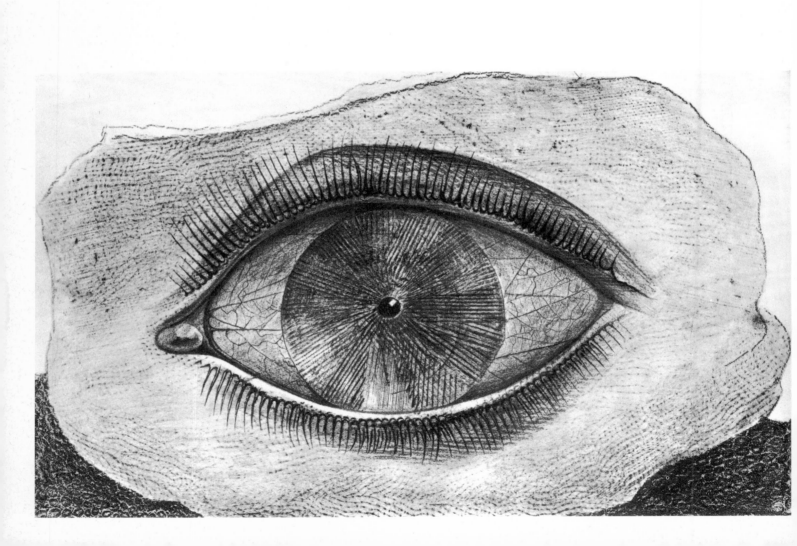

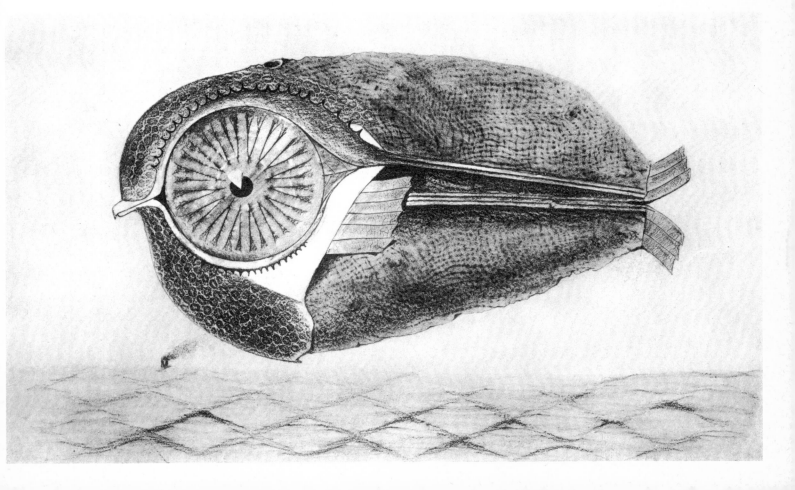

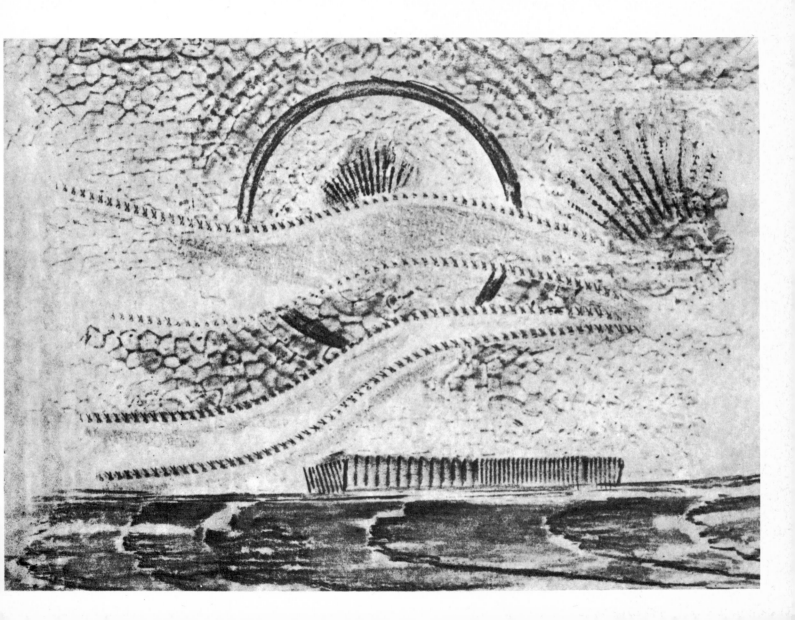

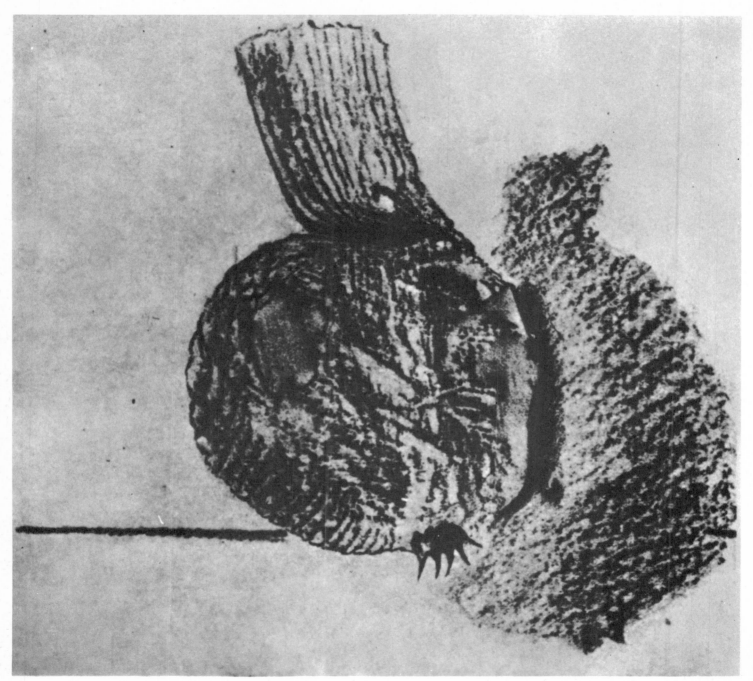

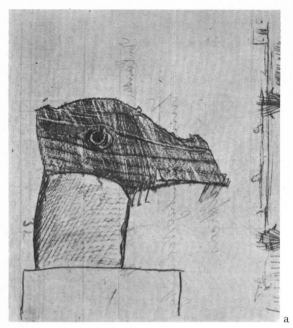

a

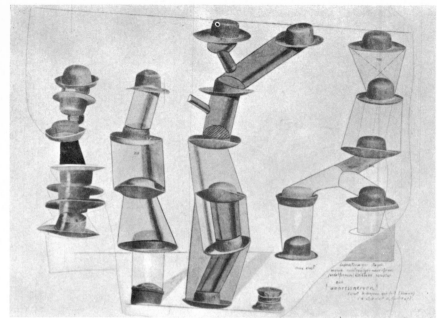

b

c

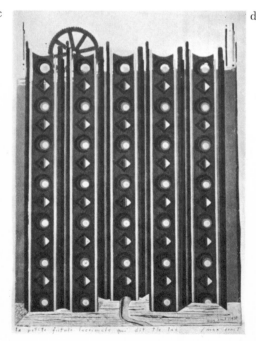

d

la petite fistule lacrimale qui dit tic tac   max ernst

a

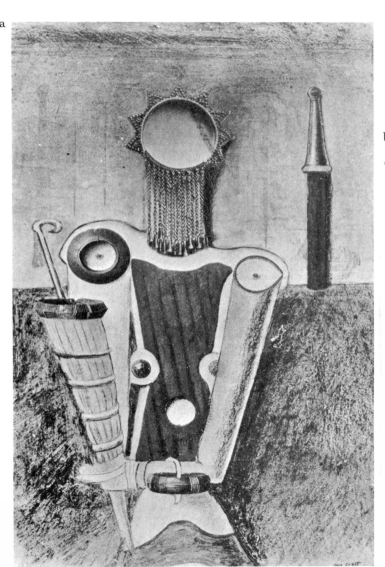

b

1905 la terre est une femme totalisie   max ernst

c

a

b

c

d

e

36

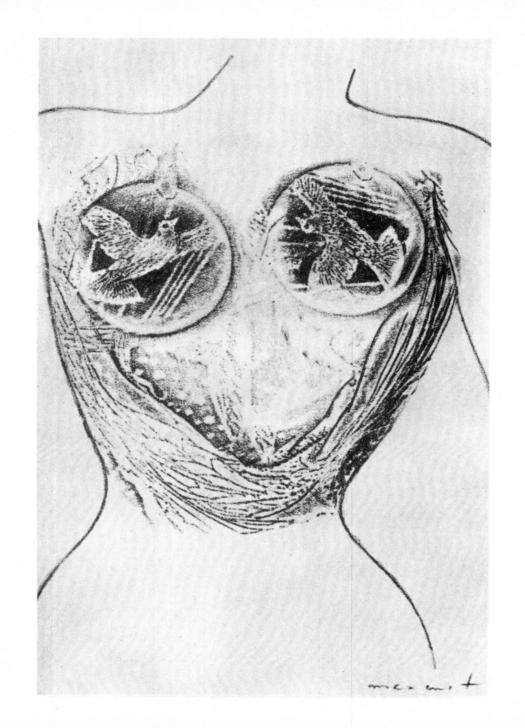

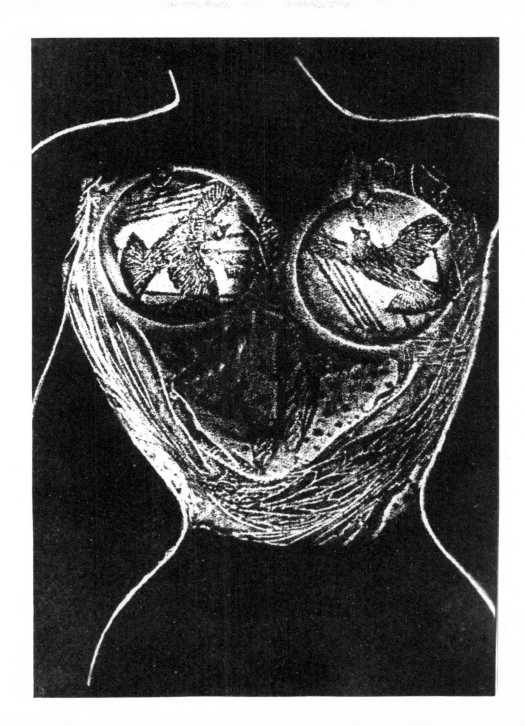

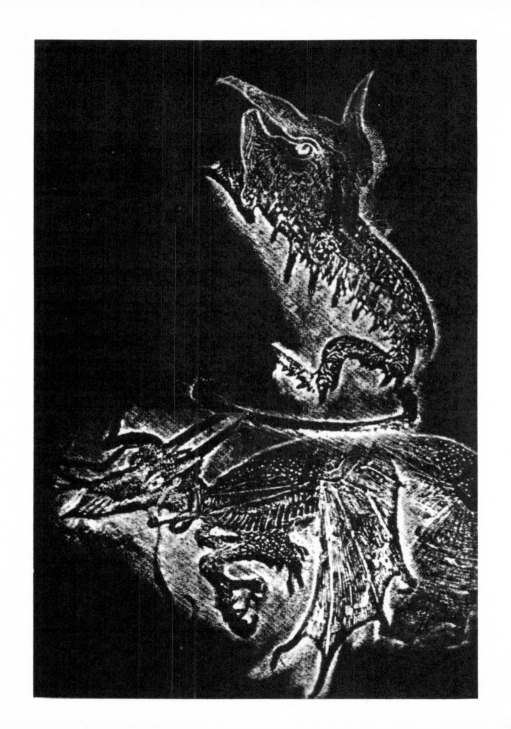

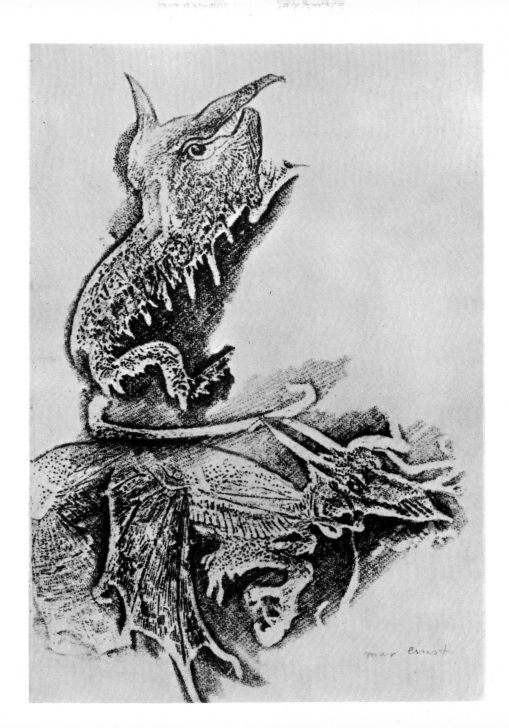

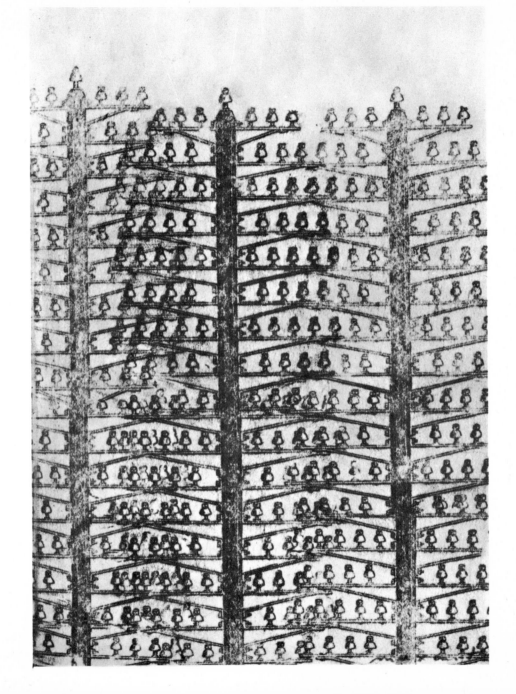

44

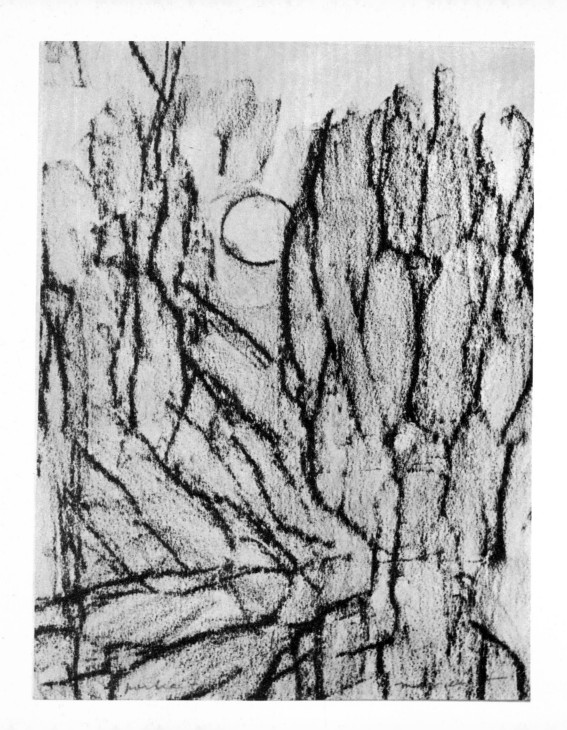

48

tête de corbeau   max ernst

49

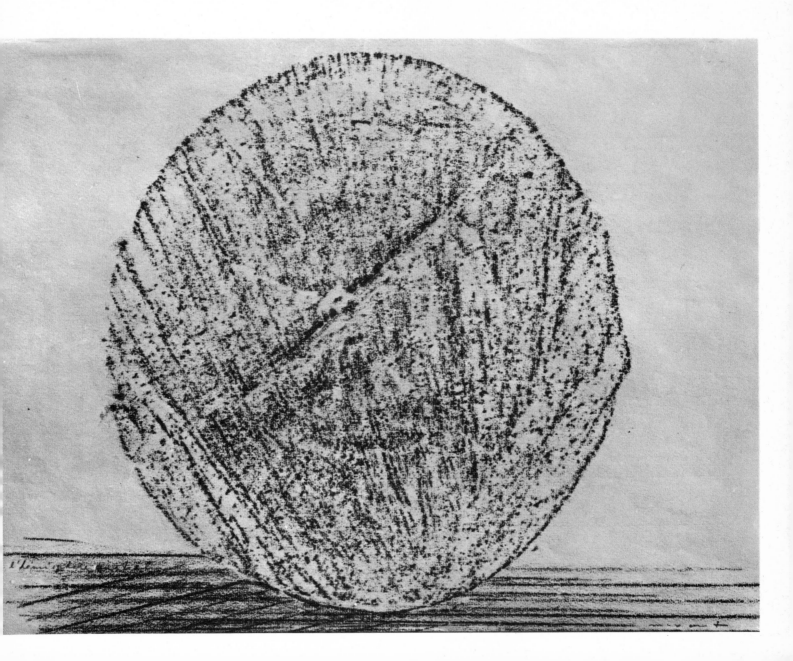

Garten mit Blick aufs Meer   max ernst 63

52

Notes

1 Ernst had gone there to avoid possible trouble, because he had signed a manifesto against France's Moroccan War.

2 "*Au-delà de la peinture*," *Cahiers d'Art*, No. 6/7, Paris, 1937.

3 For example, *Small machine constructed by minimax dadamax himself*... (reproduced in John Russell, *Max Ernst*, New York, 1967). The sheet *Erectio sine qua non* (fig. 3) is an early example of how Ernst enriched a frottage structure with a mixed technique: drawing, watercolor, and collage.

4 *Fiat Modes, Pereat Ars* is a series of eight original lithographs by Max Ernst (Cologne: Schlömilch Verlag, 1919).

5 Another frottage *avant la lettre* was created in 1921 in Tarrenz bei Imst. Ernst was spending a vacation there with Tristan Tzara and Jean Arp. André Breton later joined the group. Ernst made this frottage, *Animal* (fig. 34a), on the back of a telegram. Fascinated by the work, Tzara kept it in his collection until his death. *Animal* is a direct but crude prototype of the frottages in *Histoire Naturelle*. A comparison with the later sheets clearly shows how Ernst refined the frottage technique by his conscious use of it.

6 Leonardo da Vinci, *Treatise on Painting*. In the edition edited by him (Paris: Hermann, 1964), André Chastel makes the interesting comment that the relationship between Ernst and Leonardo should not be confined solely to this hypothesis, which interpreters of Ernst have tended to treat as an unimportant detail. Indeed, there does seem a logical progression from Leonardo's mysterious, half-arrested landscapes to Ernst's cosmological sheets. Behind Leonardo's Saint Anne trinity is revealed a cosmic vision that calls for interpretation and concerning which we can no more find an exact answer than we can for the sheets in Ernst's *Histoire Naturelle*.

7 Cf. note 2.

8 An exception must be made for Michaux' frottages. The solidified form of these works seems to relate them in content to Ernst's *Histoire Naturelle*. Ernst's frottage technique, which he used in working with lithographic transfer-paper, influenced the graphic work of Picasso and Masson.

9 Resumed in *Point du Jour* (Paris: Gallimard, 1934), pp. 217 ff.

10 The choice of titles plays a large role in Ernst's work. It follows on the heels of the artistic act of creation. Jean Arp's "*Introduction à l'Histoire Naturelle*" is a paraphrase of Ernst's title for that cycle of frottages.

11 M. Blanchot, preface to *Comte de Lautréamont: Oeuvres Complètes* (Paris: José Corti, 1963), pp. 107ff.

12 Dali defines "paranoid-critical activity" as follows: "A spontaneous method of irrational understanding, relying on the critical-interpretive association of illusory phenomena. The method enables one to interpret an object anew—not only an amorphous thing such as a cloud but every object however realistic—by becoming alienated from it."

13 Cf. note 2.

14 Ernst writes in "Au-delà de la peinture," p. 32 (see also note 2 above): "For here the two techniques that compel inspiration—frottage and collage—come together. There is such a great similarity between the two techniques that, without making many changes, I could use the description I have made of the one to tell how I discovered the other."

15 *Poème-objet* (poem-object): pictures and collages in which pictorial elements and linguistic elements (letters, exclamation points, phrases) are apprehended as a unity.

16 The composition points in the direction of Dada, to the half-ironic, half-fascinated analogies with machines. Picabia, one of whose drawings Ernst owned, exerted some influence on the works Ernst created in Cologne with his nonfunctioning apparatuses.

17 Undoubtedly this iconography of absurd machinery poked fun at man's unbounded faith in industrialization.

18 Ernst saw reproductions of De Chirico's drawings in Munich in 1919, in the magazine *Valori Plastici*. According to Ernst's own statement, *Fiat Modes, Pereat Ars* is an "homage to De Chirico."

19 *The Song of the Flesh*... (1920) is also an example of the use of photographs. (Reproduced in Russell, *Max Ernst*, New York, 1967.)

20 Patrick Waldberg, *Max Ernst* (Paris: Jean-Jacques Pauvert, 1958).

[21] Furthermore, in *La femme 100 têtes* (1929), Chapter 7, Ernst created a collage of *The Giant's Causeway*.

[22] Ernst wanted to burn the sheets omitted by Jeanne Bucher, but Paul Eluard got hold of them before they were destroyed, had them bound, and wrote his poem "Est-ce le Miroir..." for the volume. The book later fell into the hands of a Belgian art dealer who subsequently put it up for auction in Paris. Three purchasers got together and then divided the volume among themselves. The individual sheets were exhibited at the Galerie Berggruen in Paris in 1956 and at the Galerie Der Spiegel in Cologne in 1957. At present they are scattered to the four winds.

[23] Max Ernst, *Histoire Naturelle* (Cologne: Galerie Der Spiegel, 1965).

[24] In *Decalcomanias*, which Ernst did between 1937 and 1941, the level of interpretation is broader. The stereotype technique taken over from Oscar Dominguez permits of various interpretations. In pictures of that type the structure is diffuse, reminding one of moss, rotting trees, creeping vines. The frottage technique differs from this in its dry, almost crystalline precision.

[25] Subsequently Ernst used such things as zinc etchings, wallpaper, pasty oil paintings for his frottages.

[26] He uses this abruptly contrasting perspective also in *The Elephant of the Celebes* (1921).

[27] It must be borne in mind that so carefully "drawn" a sheet as *Stallion and Bride of the Wind* (fig. 25) was done without a stroke of the pencil. In this sheet Ernst created the most delicate synthesis out of rubbed threads. He had already used threads in *Whip Lashes or Lava Threads* (fig. 12) and in *Scars* (fig. 13), but not until *Stallion and Bride of the Wind* does he use the structure of the thread as a pencil stroke. These "thread frottages" found their equivalents in painting, for example in *The Horde* (1927) and in *Young People in Petrified Attitudes* (1927). Ernst painted these pictures in Mégève while on a skiing vacation. In the evening he tossed threads on the table and shaped them like a skein. He then rubbed the drawing of the thread on canvas and completed it.

[28] In Ernst's graphic works we find many examples of rubbed lithographs. Apart from individual sheets, he used this technique to illustrate the following works: Paul Eluard, *Chanson complète* (Paris: Gallimard, 1939); *Manifeste du Surréalisme*; André Breton, *Poisson Soluble*, new edition including a preface and "La Lettre aux Vogantes" (Paris: Editions Kra, 1929).

List of illustrations

The untitled illustrations scattered throughout the text were executed by the artist especially for this volume.

Illustrations pages 4–28 are part of the thirty-four engravings made for *Histoire Naturelle*. These frottages were executed in 1925 and reproduced in 1926 by photogravure, and published by Jeanne Bucher in Paris. Engraving size, $19^5/_8 \times 12^3/_4''$:

34c   Landscape to My Taste, reworked photograph, 1920

34d   The Little Tear Gland That Says Tic Tac, collage with gouache and India ink on paper, 1920, $14^1/_8 \times 10''$. The Museum of Modern Art, New York

35a   Perturbation, My Sister, collage and pencil, 1921, $9^7/_8 \times 6^1/_4''$. Collection Paul Eluard

35b   The Earth Is a Distant Woman, frottage, 1925, $4^3/_8 \times 6''$

35c   Dadaville, cork and plaster of Paris, partly painted, 1923–24, $26 \times 22''$. Collection Sir Roland Penrose, London

36a   Two Grapes, frottage, watercolor, and colored crayon on paper, 1924, $26 \times 15''$. Collection Pierre Janlet, Brussels

36b   Visible Apple, oil on canvas, 1924, $10^1/_4 \times 7^1/_8''$. Private collection

36c   The Beautiful Gardener, oil on canvas, 1923–24, $77^1/_8 \times 44^7/_8''$. Whereabouts unknown

36d   Airplane Trap, oil on canvas, 1935. Collection K. Seligmann

36e   Fire in the Forest, frottage, 1966, $15^3/_{16} \times 11^3/_8''$

37   The Marseillaise, frottage, 1931, $12^1/_4 \times 9''$

Illustrations pages 38–43 were made for René Crevel's book, *Mr. Knife and Miss Fork*, Paris, The Black Sun Press, 1931:

38   ... it is two little birds she has closed up in her dress..., frottage, 1931, $7 \times 4^1/_2''$

39   ...it is two little birds she has closed up in her dress..., Rayogramm of a Max Ernst frottage, 1931, $7 \times 4^1/_2''$

40   ...preferring above all the fabulous animals..., Rayogramm of a Max Ernst frottage, 1931, $7 \times 4^1/_2''$

41   ...preferring above all the fabulous animals..., frottage, 1931, $7 \times 4^1/_2''$

42   But at this moment the apocalyptic beast was death..., frottage, $7 \times 4^1/_2''$

43   ...that she was born in a country that you, you'll never go to..., frottage, 1931, $7 \times 4^1/_2''$

44   The Great Wall of China, frottage, 1937, $9^1/_2 \times 7^3/_4''$

46   Ghost Boat, frottage, 1962, $9^7/_8 \times 11^{15}/_{16}''$

47   Colored Frottage, 1950, $11^3/_4 \times 10^1/_4''$

48   The Portrait, frottage, 1965, $14^1/_8 \times 10''$. Private collection, Geneva

49   Head of a Raven, frottage, 1965, $17^1/_2 \times 12^1/_2''$

50   Another World, frottage, 1965, $12^5/_8 \times 12^1/_4''$. Private collection, Geneva

51   The Astral Hemisphere, frottage, 1965, $13 \times 16^1/_2''$. Private collection, Geneva

52   Garden with Seaview, frottage and collage, 1967, $12^1/_4 \times 8''$

Bibliography

There are no individual studies on the subject of the frottages.

The most exhaustive bibliography of Max Ernst's writings and of writings about Ernst is in: Max Ernst, *Beyond Painting*, New York, Wittenborn, Schultz, Inc., 1948. This bibliography, prepared by Bernard Karpel, has been brought up to date in: Jean Hugues, *Max Ernst, écrits et œuvre gravé*, Tours/Paris, 1964.

The most important recent publication is: John Russell, *Max Ernst*, New York, Harry N. Abrams, Inc., and Thames and Hudson, Ltd., London, 1967.

The editions of *Histoire Naturelle* are:

Max Ernst, *Histoire Naturelle*, Paris, Editions Jeanne Bucher, 1926. 34 sheets. The frottages are reproduced in collotype. Includes "Introduction à l'Histoire Naturelle," by Jean Arp.

Max Ernst, *Histoire Naturelle*, Paris, Jean-Jacques Pauvert, 1960. In this new edition 34 sheets have been reproduced in greatly reduced size. Contains the "Introduction" by Arp.

Max Ernst, *Histoire Naturelle*, Cologne, Galerie Der Spiegel, 1965. With 86 offset reproductions of the frottages, including 52 sheets that were not in the first edition of *Histoire Naturelle*. For this edition Ernst wrote a "Guide" and a "Commentary." Contains an unpublished poem by Paul Eluard dated 1926, as well as a German version of Arp's "Introduction."

The publishers wish to thank the Galerie Le Point Cardinal, Paris, for their co-operation in the preparation of this volume, and for the loan of photographs. For the reproductions from *Histoire Naturelle*, the author kindly furnished us with his personal set of the originals.